C000135805

THE ROYAL COURT THEATRE PRESENTS

Shoe Lady

by E.V. Crowe

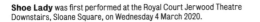

Shoe Lady was first performed at the Royal Court Jerwood Theatre
Downstairs, Sloane Square, on Wednesday 4 March 2020.

Shoe Lady
by E.V. Crowe

CAST (in order of appearance)

Viv **Katherine Parkinson**
Kenny/Curtains **Tom Kanji**
Elaine **Kayla Meikle**
Child/Tree **Archer Brandon, Beatrice White**

Director **Vicky Featherstone**
Designer **Chloe Lamford**
Lighting Designer **Natasha Chivers**
Composer **Matthew Herbert**
Sound Designer **Tony Gayle**
Movement Director **Sasha Milavic Davies**
Associate Lighting Designer **Simisola Lucia Majekodunmi**
Puppetry Consultant **Mervyn Millar**
Casting Director **Amy Ball**
Children's Casting Director **Verity Naughton**
Production Manager **Simon Evans**
Costume Supervisor **Katie Price**
Stage Manager **Lizzie Donaghy**
Deputy Stage Manager **Osnat Koblenz**
Assistant Stage Manager **Beth Absalom**
Chaperone **Sam Harrison**
Set built by **Ridiculous Solutions**

The Royal Court Theatre and Stage Management wish to thank the following for their help
with this production:
G P & J Baker Ltd.

Shoe Lady
by E.V. Crowe

E.V. Crowe (Writer)

For the Royal Court: **The Sewing Group, Hero, Kin, The Unknown (The Site Programme); Sex, Collaboration (Open Court); One Runs The Other Doesn't (Theatre Local).**

Other theatre includes: **Brenda (HighTide/Yard); I Can Hear You (RSC); Virgin (nabokov/Watford Palace); Liar Liar (Unicorn); Young Pretender (nabokov/Edinburgh Festival Fringe); Doris Day, A Just Act (Clean Break/Soho).**

Dance includes: **Live Feed/I'm Going to Show You (Siobhan Davies Dance).**

Television includes: **Pig Life (from Snatches: Moments from 100 Years of Women's Lives), Glue, Coming Up: Big Girl.**

Radio includes: **How to Say Goodbye Properly, Cry Babies, I Confess.**

Awards include: **Imison Award for Best Radio Drama Script (How to Say Goodbye Properly).**

Archer Brandon (Child/Tree)

Television includes: **Parental Guidance (Pilot), Hold the Sunset.**

Film includes: **Bloomberg Global Climate Exchange.**

Shoe Lady is Archer's professional stage debut.

Natasha Chivers (Lighting Designer)

For the Royal Court: **White Pearl, Inside Bitch (& Clean Break), The Cane, Bad Roads, Fireworks, Adler & Gibb, The Mistress Contract, Gastronauts, The Djinns of Eidgah, That Face (& West End).**

Other theatre includes: **Message in a Bottle (Sadler's Wells); Ivanov (Staatstheater Stuttgart); Blood Wedding (Young Vic); The Doctor (Almeida); The Antipodes, Sunset at the Villa Thalia, Statement of Regret (National); Allelujah (Bridge/NT Live); Oedipus (Toneelgroep, Amsterdam); The Duchess of Malfi (RSC); Sylvia (Old Vic); 1984 (West End/ Broadway); Hamlet, Oresteia (Almeida/West End); The House They Grew Up In (Chichester Festival); The Taming of the Shrew (Globe); Happy Days (Crucible, Sheffield); Green Snake (National Theatre of China); The Radicalisation of Bradley Manning (National Theatre Wales); Macbeth (& Broadway), 27, The Wolves in the Walls, Home (National Theatre of Scotland); Sunday in the Park with George (West End).**

Dance includes: **Aisha & Abhaya, International Draft Works (Royal Opera House); Belonging (Skånes Dansteater, Sweden); Strapless (Royal Ballet).**

Awards include: **Theatre Award UK for Best Design (Happy Days); Olivier Award for Best Lighting Design (Sunday in the Park with George).**

Vicky Featherstone (Director)

For the Royal Court: **all of it, On Bear Ridge [co-director] (& National Theatre Wales), The Cane, Gundog, My Mum's a Twat [co-director], Cyprus Avenue (& Abbey, Dublin/Public, NYC), Bad Roads, Victory Condition, X, How to Hold Your Breath, God Bless the Child, Maidan: Voices from the Uprising, The Mistress Contract, The Ritual Slaughter of Gorge Mastromas, Untitled Matriarch Play, The President Has Come to See You (Open Court Weekly Rep).**

Other theatre includes: **What if Women Ruled the World? (Manchester International Festival); Our Ladies of Perpetual Succour (& Live/ National/West End/International tour), Enquirer [co-director], An Appointment with the Wicker Man, 27, The Wheel, Somersaults, Wall of Death: A Way of Life [co-director], Cockroach (& Traverse), 365 (& Edinburgh International Festival), Mary Stuart (& Citizens/Royal Lyceum, Edinburgh), The Wolves in the Walls [co-director] (& Tramway/Lyric, Hammersmith/UK tour/New Victory, NYC), The Miracle Man, Empty, Long Gone Lonesome (National Theatre of Scotland); The Small Things, Pyrenees, On Blindness, The Drowned World, Tiny Dynamite, Crazy Gary's Mobile Disco, Splendour, Riddance, The Cosmonaut's Last Message to the Woman He Once Loved in the Former Soviet Union, Crave (Paines Plough).**

Television includes: **Pritilata (from Snatches: Moments from 100 Years of Women's Lives), Where the Heart Is, Silent Witness.**

Film includes: **Climate Change: what do you want me to say? (Royal Court/Financial Times short film), Cyprus Avenue (The Space/BBC capture).**

Vicky was Artistic Director of Paines Plough 1997–2005 and the inaugural Artistic Director of the National Theatre of Scotland 2005–2012. She is Artistic Director of the Royal Court.

Tony Gayle (Sound Designer)

For the Royal Court: **Poet in da Corner.**

Other theatre includes: **Beautiful – The Carole King Musical, Jersey Boys, Salad Days, American Idiot (UK tour); Songs For Nobodies (& West End), Floyd Collins (Wilton's Music Hall); The Wild Party (Other Palace); Lazarus (King's Cross); West Side Story (Bishopsgate Institute); Godspell (West End).**

As associate sound designer, theatre includes: **Dear Evan Hansen (West End); Tina – The Tina Turner Musical (West End/Hamburg/Utrecht); The Book of Mormon (West End/European tour); Disney's Aladdin (West End/Germany); The Girl from the North Country, Groundhog Day (Old Vic); Matilda The Musical (International tour).**

Awards include: **British Black Theatre Recognition Award.**

Matthew Herbert (Composer)

As composer, for the Royal Court: **Gundog, Drunk Enough to Say I Love You?**

As composer & sound designer, for the Royal Court: **The Unknown (The Site Programme).**

As composer, other theatre includes: **People Places & Things (National); Fatherland (Manchester International Festival); Machinal (Broadway).**

As writer, theatre includes: **The Hush (National).**

As writer, opera includes: **The Crackle (Royal Opera House).**

As composer, film includes: **A Fantastic Woman, The Cave, Gloria Bell, Disobedience.**

As author, fiction includes: **The Music.**

Matthew is an award-winning composer, artist, producer and writer whose work extends from numerous albums, remixes and film scores to music for theatre, television, video games and radio. He has produced multiple artists and released many of them on his own record label, Accidental Records.

Tom Kanji (Kenny/Curtains)

Theatre includes: **Yes Prime Minister (Theatr Clwyd); A Midsummer Night's Dream, Macbeth (Shakespeare's Rose); Richard III (Headlong); Love's Labour's Lost, The Winter's Tale, Pericles, Romeo & Juliet, Julius Caesar, Doctor Scroggy's War, Eternal Love (Globe); The Country Wife (Chichester Festival); The Taming of the Shrew (US tour); Box of Delights (Wilton's Music Hall); Fiddler on the Roof, Romeo & Juliet, The Story Giant, The Sum (Everyman, Liverpool); Romeo & Juliet, Anthony & Cleopatra, Much Ado About Nothing (Barbican); Cadfael – The Virgin in the Ice (Middle Ground); Much Ado About Nothing,**
Twelfth Night (Ludlow Festival); A Russian Play (Lion & Unicorn); Hamlet (Northern Broadsides); Othello, The Importance of Being Earnest (QM2); Wild Horses (Theatre503); Back of the Throat (Old Red Lion); The Girl, the Oil Pipe & the Murder in the Forum, The Tempest (Tara Arts); Prints of Denmark (Edinburgh Festival Fringe); Les Liaisons Dangereuses (New Vic, Stoke); Indian Ink (Salisbury Playhouse).**

Television includes: **Tyrant, Silent Witness, Hustle, Midnight Man, Saddam's Tribe.**

Chloe Lamford (Designer)

For the Royal Court: **Superhoe [as design consultant], The Song Project [& co-creator], The Cane, Pity, Gundog, My Mum's a Twat, Grimly Handsome [& co-creator], The Site Programme, Victory Condition, B, Road, Nuclear War, Unreachable, Ophelia's Zimmer (& Schaubühne, Berlin), How to Hold Your Breath, God Bless the Child, 2071, Teh Internet Is Serious Business, Open Court 2013, Circle Mirror Transformation.**

Other theatre includes: **The Antipodes [& co-director], John, Amadeus, Rules for Living, The World of Extreme Happiness (National); Europe, Teenage Dick, The Tempest, Salt Root & Roe (Donmar); The American Clock (Old Vic); Hilary & Clinton (Broadway); The Crucible (Theater Basel); TBCTV (Somerset House); Hamilton Complex (Schauspielhaus, Bochum); 1984 (& Headlong/West End/Broadway), The Duchess of Malfi (Almeida); The Maids (Toneelgroep, Amsterdam); Shakespeare's Last Play, Atmen (Schaubühne, Berlin); Our Ladies of Perpetual Succour (& Live/National/West End/International tour), My Shrinking Life, An Appointment with the Wicker Man, Knives in Hens (National Theatre of Scotland); Britney & Goofy, Het Hamiltoncomplex (Hetpaleis, Antwerp); The Events (& ATC), Disco Pigs, Sus, Blackta [costume] (Young Vic); Praxis Makes Perfect, The Radicalisation of Bradley Manning (National Theatre Wales); Boys (Headlong/Soho); Jubilee, Cannibals (Royal Exchange, Manchester); The History Boys (Crucible, Sheffield); it felt empty when the heart went at first but it is alright now (Clean Break/Arcola); This Wide Night (Soho).**

Opera & dance includes: **Verklärte Nacht (Rambert/Kim Brandstrup); Miranda (Opera Comique, Paris); Ariadne Auf Naxos, Alcina, Pelleas & Melisande (Aix-en-Provence Festival); The Little Sweep, Let's Make an Opera (Malmo Opera House, Sweden); The Magic Flute (English Touring Opera); War & Peace (Scottish Opera/RCS).**

Awards include: **Arts Foundation Fellowship Award for Design for Performance in Set & Costume, Theatrical Management Association Award for Best Theatre Design (Small Miracle).**

Chloe is Associate Designer at the Royal Court.

Simisola Lucia Majekodunmi
(Associate Lighting Designer)

As lighting designer, theatre includes: **Transformations (New Public); J'ouvert (Theatre503); Driving Miss Daisy, Baby Box (Theatre Royal, York); Invisible Harmony (Southbank Centre).**

Kayla Meikle (Elaine)

For the Royal Court: **ear for eye, Primetime.**

Other theatre includes: **All My Sons (Old Vic); Vassa, Dance Nation (Almeida); A Midsummer Night's Dream, Jack & the Beanstalk (Lyric, Hammersmith); I Have a Mouth & I Will Scream, People Who Need People, Streets (VAULT Festival); Macbeth, Romeo & Juliet (National); The Taming of the Shrew (Arts); Merlin (Nuffield); All That Lives (Ovalhouse).**

Television includes: **Small Axe, Afterlife, Will.**

Film includes: **Morning Song, Soundproof, State Zero, Every Eight Minutes, Samira's Party.**

Sasha Milavic Davies
(Movement Director)

As movement director, for the Royal Court: **Pity.**

As movement director, other theatre includes: **Touching the Void (West End); Antipodes (National); Our Town (Regent's Park Open Air); Berberian Sound Studio (Donmar).**

As choreographer, theatre includes: **The Merry Wives of Windsor (Globe); The Writer (Almeida); Jubilee (Royal Exchange, Manchester/Lyric, Hammersmith); The Suppliant Women (Royal Lyceum, Edinburgh/ATC/Young Vic).**

As director, theatre includes: **YV Unpacked: She ventures and He wins (Young Vic); Pet Života Pretužnog Milutina, Moja Ti, Constellations (Atelje 212, Serbia); One Side to the Other [installation] (Akram Khan Company/The Lowry).**

As choreographer, dance & opera includes: **Everything That Rises Must Dance (Complicité/Dance Umbrella); La Bianca Notte (Hamburg Opera); Von Heute Auf Morgen, Sancta Susana (Opera de Lyon).**

As associate director, opera includes: **The Wasp Factory (& Bregenz, Austria/Hebbel am Ufer, Berlin), The Crackle (Royal Opera House).**

Awards include: **Muci Draškic Award for Best Director (Constellations/Moja Ti).**

Sasha works as a movement director, choreographer, director and dramaturg. She was a founding member and Artistic Associate of the Yard Theatre and was part of Festival d'Avignon's Voyages de Kadmos programme for emerging artists.

Mervyn Millar (Puppetry Consultant)

As puppet designer/director, for the Royal Court: **Get Santa!**

Other theatre includes: **Circus 1903 (Southbank Centre/International tour); As You Like It, Great Expectations, The Comedy of Errors (RSC); The Lion, the Witch & the Wardrobe (Birmingham Rep); Peter Pan, Die Brüder Löwenherz (Schauspielhaus, Zürich); James II (National Theatre of Scotland); Stiller (Residenz Munich); Crow (Handspring UK); Wo De Xiao Huo Ban (Xi'an, China); The Odyssey (Lyric, Hammersmith/Bristol Old Vic).**

Opera includes: **Siegfried, Die Walküre (Opera National du Rhin).**

Music videos include: **Appreciate (Paul McCartney).**

Mervyn is a director and puppetry specialist. He was part of the original creative team of the National Theatre's *War Horse*, also appearing at the National and directing casts in London, New York, Toronto and Berlin. *Evidence for the Existence of Borrowers* (a collaboration with Kazuko Hohki and Andy Cox) won a Total Theatre Award and Herald Angel Award. His books include *Puppetry: How to Do It, The Horse's Mouth* and *The Journey of The Tall Horse*. In 2010 he was awarded an Arts Foundation Fellowship for his work in puppetry.

Katherine Parkinson (Viv)

For the Royal Court: **Cock, The Seagull.**

Other theatre includes: **Uncle Vanya (Theatre Royal, Bath); Home, I'm Darling (& National), Dead Funny, Absent Friends (West End); Before the Party (Almeida); The School for Scandal (Barbican); Other Hands (Soho); The Age of Consent (Bush).**

Television includes: **Defending the Guilty, Humans, The Honourable Woman, Inside No. 9, In the Club, The IT Crowd, Whites, The Old Guys, Doc Martin.**

Film includes: **This Nan's Life, Paul Dood's Deadly Lunchbreak, Radioactive, Guernsey, The Boat that Rocked, Easy Virtue.**

Beatrice White (Child/Tree)

Theatre includes: **Cat On a Hot Tin Roof (Young Vic).**

Television includes: **The Child in Time, Nickelodeon Junior.**

THE ROYAL COURT THEATRE

The Royal Court Theatre is the writers' theatre. It is a leading force in world theatre for cultivating and supporting writers – undiscovered, emerging and established.

Through the writers, the Royal Court is at the forefront of creating restless, alert, provocative theatre about now. We open our doors to the unheard voices and free thinkers that, through their writing, change our way of seeing.

Over 120,000 people visit the Royal Court in Sloane Square, London, each year and many thousands more see our work elsewhere through transfers to the West End and New York, UK and international tours, digital platforms, our residencies across London, and our site-specific work. Through all our work we strive to inspire audiences and influence future writers with radical thinking and provocative discussion.

The Royal Court's extensive development activity encompasses a diverse range of writers and artists and includes an ongoing programme of writers' attachments, readings, workshops and playwriting groups. Twenty years of the International Department's pioneering work around the world means the Royal Court has relationships with writers on every continent.

Since 1956 we have commissioned and produced hundreds of writers, from John Osborne to Jasmine Lee-Jones. Royal Court plays from every decade are now performed on stage and taught in classrooms and universities across the globe.

We're now working to the future and are committed to becoming a carbon net zero arts venue throughout 2020 to ensure we can continue to work for generations of writers and audiences to come.

It is because of this commitment to the writer and our future that we believe there is no more important theatre in the world than the Royal Court.

**Find out more at
royalcourttheatre.com**

  royalcourt ▌ royalcourttheatre

ROYAL

COMING UP AT THE ROYAL COURT

2 – 25 Apr

Rare Earth Mettle
By Al Smith
Generously supported with a lead gift from Charles Holloway. Recipient of an Edgerton Foundation New Play Award. Supported by Cockayne Grant for the Arts, a donor advised fund of The London Community Foundation.

9 Apr – 9 May

two Palestinians go dogging
By Sami Ibrahim
Royal Court Theatre and Theatre Uncut

7 – 16 May

The Song Project
Concept by Chloe Lamford and Wende

Created by Chloe Lamford, Wende, Isobel Waller-Bridge and Imogen Knight

With words by E.V. Crowe, Sabrina Mahfouz, Somalia Seaton, Stef Smith and Debris Stevenson

20 May – 20 Jun

A Fight Against...
By Pablo Manzi
Translated by William Gregory
Royal Court Theatre and Teatro a Mil Foundation
The development of A FIGHT AGAINST... was supported by the British Council.

29 May - 3 Jul

The Glow
By Alistair McDowall

29 Jun - 11 Jul

Purple Snowflakes and Titty Wanks
By Sarah Hanly
Royal Court Theatre and Abbey Theatre

20 Jul - 15 Aug

Is God Is
By Aleshea Harris

21 Jul - 1 Aug

Nanjing
By Jude Christian
Royal Court Theatre and Tamara Moore

royalcourttheatre.com

Sloane Square London, SW1W 8AS
⊖ Sloane Square ⇄ Victoria Station
🐦 royalcourt 📘 theroyalcourttheatre 📷 royalcourttheatre

ASSISTED PERFORMANCES

Captioned Performances

Captioned performances are accessible for D/deaf, deafened & hard of hearing people as well as being suitable for people for whom English is not a first language. There are regular captioned performances in the Jerwood Theatre Downstairs on Wednesdays and the Jerwood Theatre Upstairs on Fridays.

In the Jerwood Theatre Downstairs
Rare Earth Mettle: Wed 22 Apr, 7.30pm
The Glow: Wed 17, 24 Jun & 1 July, 7.30pm
Is God Is: Wed 5 & 12 Aug, 7.30pm

In the Jerwood Theatre Upstairs
two Palestinians go dogging: Fri 24 Apr, 1 & 8 May, 7.45pm
A Fight Against...: Fri 5, 12 & 19 Jun, 7.45pm

Audio Described Performances

Audio described performances are accessible for blind or partially sighted customers. They are preceded by a touch tour (at 1pm) which allows patrons access to elements of theatre design including set and costume.

In the Jerwood Theatre Downstairs
Rare Earth Mettle: Sat 25 Apr, 2.30pm
The Glow: Sat 27 Jun, 2.30pm
Is God Is: Sat 8 Aug, 2.30pm

ROYAL

ASSISTED PERFORMANCES

Performances in a Relaxed Environment

Relaxed Environment performances are suitable for those who may benefit from a more relaxed experience.

During these performances:
- There will be a relaxed attitude to noise in the auditorium; you are welcome to respond to the show in whatever way feels natural
- You can enter and exit the auditorium when needed
- We will help you find the best seats
- House lights remained raised slightly
- Loud noises may be reduced

In the Jerwood Theatre Downstairs
Rare Earth Mettle: Sat 18 Apr, 2.30pm
The Glow: Sat 13 Jun, 2.30pm
Is God Is: Sat 1 Aug, 2.30pm

In the Jerwood Theatre Upstairs
two Palestinians go dogging: Sat 2 May, 3pm
A Fight Against...: Sat 20 Jun, 3pm

If you would like to talk to us about your access requirements please contact our Box Office at (0)20 7565 5000 or **boxoffice@royalcourttheatre.com** The Royal Court Visual Story is available on our website. We also produce Story Synopsis and Sensory Synopsis which are available on request.

For more information and to book access tickets online, visit

royalcourttheatre.com/access

Sloane Square London, SW1W 8AS ⊖ Sloane Square ⇌ Victoria Station
🐦 royalcourt 📘 theroyalcourttheatre 📷 royalcourttheatre

COURT

ROYAL COURT SUPPORTERS

The Royal Court is a registered charity and not-for-profit company. We need to raise £1.5 million every year in addition to our core grant from the Arts Council and our ticket income to achieve what we do.

We have significant and longstanding relationships with many generous organisations and individuals who provide vital support. Royal Court supporters enable us to remain the writers' theatre, find stories from everywhere and create theatre for everyone.

We can't do it without you.

PUBLIC FUNDING

Arts Council England, London
British Council

TRUSTS & FOUNDATIONS

The Derrill Allatt Foundation
The Backstage Trust
The Boshier-Hinton Foundation
Martin Bowley Charitable Trust
The Chapman Charitable Trust
CHK Foundation
The City Bridge Trust
The Cleopatra Trust
Cockayne - Grants for the Arts
The Ernest Cook Trust
The Nöel Coward Foundation
Cowley Charitable Trust
The D'oyly Carte Charitable Trust
Edgerton Foundation
The Eranda Rothschild Foundation
Lady Antonia Fraser for The Pinter Commission
The Golden Bottle Trust
The Haberdashers' Company
The Paul Hamlyn Foundation
Roderick & Elizabeth Jack
Jerwood Arts
The Leche Trust
The Andrew Lloyd Webber Foundation
The London Community Foundation
John Lyon's Charity
Clare McIntyre's Bursary
The Austin & Hope Pilkington Trust
Old Possum's Practical Trust
The David & Elaine Potter Foundation
The Richard Radcliffe Charitable Trust
Rose Foundation
Royal Victoria Hall Foundation
The Sobell Foundation
John Thaw Foundation
The Garfield Weston Foundation
The Victoria Wood Foundation

CORPORATE SPONSORS

Aqua Financial Limited
Cadogan
Colbert
Edwardian Hotels, London
Fever-Tree
Greene King
Kirkland & Ellis International LLP
Kudos
MAC

CORPORATE MEMBERS

Platinum
Auriens

Gold
Weil, Gotshal & Manges LLP

Silver
Azteca Latin Lounge
Bloomberg
Kekst CNC
Left Bank Pictures
The No 8 Partnership Dental Practice
PATRIZIA
Royal Bank of Canada - Global Asset Management
Tetragon Financial Group

COMMISSION PARTNERS
Oberon Books

For more information or to become a foundation or business supporter contact: support@royalcourttheatre. com/020 7565 5064.

Supported using public funding by
ARTS COUNCIL ENGLAND

INDIVIDUAL SUPPORTERS

Artistic Director's Circle
Eric Abraham
Carolyn Bennett
Samantha & Richard
  Campbell-Breeden
Cas Donald
Jane Featherstone
Lydia & Manfred Gorvy
Jean & David Grier
Charles Holloway
Jack & Linda Keenan
Mandeep & Sarah Manku
Anatol Orient
Theo & Barbara Priovolos
NoraLee & Jon Sedmak
Deborah Shaw
  & Stephen Marquardt
Matthew & Sian Westerman
Mahdi Yahya
Anonymous

Writers' Circle
G & O Al-Qattan
Chris & Alison Cabot
Virginia Finegold
Chris Hogbin
Nicola Kerr
Héloïse & Duncan
  Matthews QC
Emma O'Donoghue
Tracy Phillips
Suzanne Pirret
Andrew & Ariana Rodger
Carol Sellars
Jan & Michael Topham
Maureen & Tony Wheeler
Anonymous

Directors' Circle
Ms Sophia Arnold
Dr Kate Best
Katie Bradford
Piers Butler
Sir Trevor & Lady Chinn
Professor John Collinge
Joachim Fleury
Julian & Ana Garel-Jones
Louis Greig
Dr Timothy Hyde
Roderick & Elizabeth Jack
Mrs Joan Kingsley
Victoria Leggett
Sir Paul & Lady Ruddock
Anonymous

Platinum Members
Moira Andreae
Nick Archdale
Tyler Bollier
Anthony Burton CBE
Clive & Helena Butler
Gavin & Lesley Casey
Sarah & Philippe Chappatte
Andrea & Anthony Coombs
Clyde Cooper
Victoria Corcoran
Andrew & Amanda Cryer
Matthew Dean
Sarah Denning
Caroline Diamond
The Drabble Family
Robyn Durie
Mark & Sarah Evans
Sally & Giles Everist
Celeste Fenichel
Emily Fletcher
The Edwin Fox Foundation
Dominic & Claire Freemantle
Beverley Gee
Nick & Julie Gould
The Richard Grand Foundation
Jill Hackel & Andrzej Zarzycki
Carol Hall
Sam & Caroline Haubold
Madeleine Hodgkin
Mr & Mrs Gordon Holmes
Soyar Hopkinson
Damien Hyland
Amanda & Chris Jennings
Ralph Kanter
Jim & Wendy Karp
David P Kaskel
  & Christopher A Teano
Vincent & Amanda Keaveny
Peter & Maria Kellner
Mr & Mrs Pawel Kisielewski
Christopher Marek Rencki
Emma Marsh
Mrs Janet Martin
Andrew McIver
David & Elizabeth Miles
Jameson & Lauren Miller
Barbara Minto
M.E. Murphy Altschuler
Siobhan Murphy
Sarah Muscat
Liv Nilssen
Andrea & Hilary Ponti
Greg & Karen Reid
Corinne Rooney
William & Hilary Russell
Sally & Anthony Salz
João Saraiva e Silva
Anita Scott
Bhags Sharma
Dr. Wendy Sigle
Paul & Rita Skinner
Brian Smith
Kim Taylor-Smith

Mrs Caroline Thomas
The Ulrich Family
Monica B Voldstad
Anne-Marie Williams
Sir Robert & Lady Wilson
Anonymous

With thanks to our Friends, Silver and Gold Supporters whose help we greatly appreciate.

DEVELOPMENT COUNCIL

Chris Cabot
Cas Donald
Sally Everist
Celeste Fenichel
Virginia Finegold
Tim Hincks
Anatol Orient
Andrew Rodger
Sian Westerman

Our Supporters contribute to all aspects of the Royal Court's work including: productions, commissions, writers' groups, International, Participation and Young Court, creative posts and access initiatives as well as providing in-kind support.

For more information or to become a Supporter please contact: support@ royalcourttheatre.com/ 020 7565 5049.

ROYAL

BAR & KITCHEN

The Royal Court's Bar & Kitchen aims to create a welcoming and inspiring environment with a style and ethos that reflects the work we put on stage. Our menu consists of simple, ingredient driven and flavour-focused dishes with an emphasis on freshness and seasonality. This is supported by a carefully curated drinks list notable for its excellent wine selection, craft beers and skilfully prepared coffee. By day a perfect spot for long lunches, meetings or quiet reflection and by night an atmospheric, vibrant meeting space for cast, crew, audiences and the general public.

GENERAL OPENING HOURS
Monday – Friday: 10am – late
Saturday: 11am – late

Advance booking is suggested at peak times.

For more information, visit
royalcourttheatre.com/bar

HIRES & EVENTS

The Royal Court is available to hire for celebrations, rehearsals, meetings, filming, ceremonies and much more. Our two theatre spaces can be hired for conferences and showcases, and the building is a unique venue for bespoke weddings and receptions.

For more information, visit
royalcourttheatre.com/events

Sloane Square London, SW1W 8AS ⊖ Sloane Square ⇌ Victoria Station
🐦 royalcourt 🅵 theroyalcourttheatre 📷 royalcourttheatre

COURT

"There are no spaces, no rooms in my opinion, with a greater legacy of fearlessness, truth and clarity than this space."

Simon Stephens, Playwright

The Royal Court invests in the future of the theatre, offering writers the support, time and resources to find their voices and tell their stories, asking the big questions and responding to the issues of the moment.

As a registered charity, the Royal Court needs to raise at least £1.5 million every year in addition to our Arts Council funding and ticket income, to keep seeking out, developing and nurturing new voices. Please join us by donating today.

You can donate online at **royalcourttheatre.com/donate** or via our **donation box in the Bar & Kitchen.**

We can't do it without you.

Support the Court

To find out more about the different ways in which you can be involved please contact support@royalcourttheatre.com/ 020 7565 5049

The English Stage Company at the Royal Court Theatre is a registered charity (No. 231242).

Shoe Lady

E.V. Crowe's plays include *The Sewing Group*, *Hero*, *Kin*, *The Unknown* (Royal Court), *Sex*, *Collaboration* (Royal Court Open Court), *Brenda* (HighTide/Yard), *I Can Hear You* (RSC), *Virgin* (nabokov/Watford Palace), *Liar Liar* (Unicorn), *Young Pretender* (nabokov/ Edinburgh Festival Fringe), *Doris Day* and *A Just Act* (Clean Break/Soho).

by the same author
from Faber

KIN
HERO
THE SEWING GROUP

E.V. CROWE

Shoe Lady

FABER & FABER

First published in 2020
by Faber and Faber Limited
74–77 Great Russell Street
London WC1B 3DA

Typeset by Brighton Gray
Printed and bound in the UK by CPI Group (Ltd), Croydon CR0 4YY

A CIP record for this book
is available from the British Library

978-0-571-35809-0

MIX
Paper from
responsible sources
FSC® C020471

2 4 6 8 10 9 7 5 3 1

For Katie and Sarah, my sisters.

Acknowledgements

I would like to thank everyone at the Royal Court Theatre, especially Vicky Featherstone. I would also like to thank: Jess Sykes and Georgia Kanner at Independent; Dinah Wood, Steve King and Jodi Gray at Faber; Laura Lomas, Tamzin Golding, Lucy Morrison, Erik Hovland, and all the other artists and friends and family who make it possible to keep writing with their encouragement and generosity.

I would like to acknowledge that the story of nothing was inspired by an anecdote told to me by the playwright and poet Dalia Taha. It really stuck in my mind, made me laugh, and I'm grateful to be able to build on it in this story.

I wrote this play in the summer of 2018. I had stopped finding the idea of being middle class a joke. I realised there was an idea of comfort that was not the experience of most middle-class people I knew, and that even basic needs – decent housing, outside space, a place to clean clothes, access to time with family, education, health, stability and rest – felt out of reach. And if the 'middle-class' experience was this, I wondered if now only the very rich had access to things we used to consider basic needs. And that one way or another this slippage across the economic divides of course affected women's lives and 'choices' the most, and made invisible those with even fewer choices. I wondered if I were about to die, what would I want to have written, and this play came to me like a song to myself in the dark.

Shoe Lady was first performed at the Royal Court Jerwood Theatre Downstairs, London, on 4 March 2020. The cast was as follows:

Viv Katherine Parkinson
Kenny/Curtains Tom Kanji
Elaine Kayla Meikle
Child/Tree Archer Brandon, Beatrice White

Director Vicky Featherstone
Designer Chloe Lamford
Lighting Designer Natasha Chivers
Composer Matthew Herbert
Sound Designer Tony Gayle
Movement Director Sasha Milavic Davies

Characters

Viv
Kenny
Elaine
Child

Curtains 1
Curtains 2
Tree

SHOE LADY

*To understand my new state of mind, however, you have
to know that I believe myself to be writing a book on
economic theory which will largely revolutionise not I
suppose at once but in the course of the next ten years the
way the world thinks about economic problems. When
my new theory has been duly assimilated and mixed with
politics and feelings and passions, I cannot predict what
the final upshot will be in its effect on actions and affairs,
but there will be a great change and in particular the
Ricardian Foundations of Marxism will be knocked away.*

*I can't expect you or anyone else to believe this at the
present stage, but for myself I don't merely hope what I
say. In my own mind I am quite sure.*

John Maynard Keynes to George Bernard Shaw,
1 January 1935

The play, as published, may differ from its presentation in performance. The production may contain changes to some lines, the order of scenes, or include additional material.

A bed.
   Viv sits upright.
   There's a lump next to her. It's Kenny. Her husband.
   He doesn't move.

Viv That's it.
   Morning!
   Good morning!
   He's up.
   I can hear him.
   Can't you?
   I can hear him.
   He's roaring like a lion.
   I'll go to him.

   She goes and comes back.

He's sitting in his chair waiting for breakfast.
   Can you go.
   Can't you go.
   You said you would.
   It's your turn.
   He's banging his spoon.
   Shreddies he's after.
   Can't you go.
   You go can't you.
   Can't you.
   Won't you go.
   It's only fair.
   Isn't it.
   Your go.

You go.
Go. Go please.
You –
You –
I won't say it but it rhymes with something.

Kenny goes.
> *Viv sits on the bed.*

I dread opening that curtain.
I dread it.
It's loose at the top. It's going to come down on me
And then what?
I'll have to put it back up.
I'll have to stand on a chair.
Or get a new one.
Or get a new one and pay someone to come and put it up.
Or get Kenny to. But then he fucks it up and I have to do it.
Myself.
Or get a new one and then pay someone to do it.
I don't know anyone handy.
It must be hard to be a man who's not handy.
It must be a burden.
Wish I was more handy.
That curtain is nigh.
Its end is nigh.
Fucking hell.
I'll risk it. Shall I?
No way.
What day is it?
Tuesday.

She pulls the curtain open. The runner collapses and the curtain ends up on the floor.

Bright light though.
 That's bright for Tuesday.
 Bright!
 Glorious dazzling bright.
 So that's good.
 I knew the curtain would get me.
 I took the risk knowingly.
 I've been in battle with that curtain.
 The curtain's won.

The curtain slides itself onto the bed next to her.

I can't believe I'm still wearing this T-shirt.
 It was Kenny's from when he was a kid.
 It's disgusting.
 I look disgusting.
 There's no time to even run a brush through my hair.
 No time to put a tampon in.
 No time to really look at myself.
 I miss vanity.
 The amount of time I used to spend looking at myself.
 Heaven.
 I long for vanity.
 I can't take being touched by the hairdresser or a
manicure person or massage person.
 No way.
 It's too erotic.
 I'd orgasm. On the spot.
 Everyone except Kenny.
 I only trust him.
 Totally unerotic.
 Joke.

*The curtain starts to smooth her hair but ends up
making it more of a mess.*

That curtain.
    What am I going to do about it?
    I don't feel I can go to work now.
    Better had.

    She stays on the bed.

You don't have to shower every day
    That's a myth.

    The curtain half covers her.

It's bright for a Tuesday.
    Got to get on.
    Get us both to work.
    Get him to school.
    Get us off and going.
    But it's the curtain I can't stop thinking about.
    I can't go to work with that down there.

    She tries to put it back up.
        Stands on a chair.
        It's a real struggle.

Lopsided curtains make me want to weep.
    How can I leave with the bed unmade and
    The curtains lopsided?
    What kind of person does that make me?
    A mess.
    A chaotic.
    Not fit for work.
    Not fit to be a mother.
    With your lopsided curtains.
    Fix it, fix it and then you can go.
    You can go and work.

    Kenny comes in.

I can't go until I've fixed this.
    I can't.

You go or you'll miss your bus.
Don't you have your meeting today?
Are they going to tell you?
What are they going to say?
More redundancies?
They can't!
I don't think so.
Let me know will you.
Don't let me know.
Tell me when I get home.

You take him to school.
I can't.
The curtain.
I can't leave it.
I can't leave it on the floor.
I'll be late for work.
I have to.
I can't be a person who goes to work and at home,
back at the house
There are curtains lying on the floor.

Kenny goes.
Viv lies down next to the curtain.

God knows where I got these from.
I'd wash them but they'll fall apart.
Faded glory or what.
Still I'm keen on them.
They're how the rest of the place should be.
They speak to me.
They matter. They are to my taste.
They are not practical.
Death to practical
Death to utilitarian.
Liberation is uselessness, I'm sure of it.
Poor curtains.

This means
    This means chaos afoot.
    This means I'm not doing my best
    I'm not bucking up.
    Not trying hard enough.
    If I was someone else and I saw me, this new person
    With curtains in this sort of state,
    I'd think – your life is not in order.
    Buck up.

The curtain starts to stroke her.
    Viv shudders.
    She pulls the curtain up.
    Half pins it up.

I feel connected to the curtains.
    To their well-being.
    Lopsided.
    I'm sorry I've let you down.
    Why does work have to matter more than curtains?
    I'll just tell them what happened.

Hi. It's Viv. Sorry I'm running a bit late today. All the
trains were delayed for some reason.
    But I'm on my way.

I'm just running out the door. Right now.

Bye.

Bye-bye curtains.

Curtain Bye.

She goes and then comes back.
    She looks at the curtain for ages.
    Touches it.
    It falls down.
    She sits on the bed.
    Puts on her shoes.

Viv One two, buckle my shoe.
Three four, knock at the door.

A tree.

Viv It's a buckle-up.
　　It's got a buckle on the strap, it must have broken.
　　I don't know
　　How I
　　How I
　　How I didn't notice.
　　It's the rush hour.
　　I just got swept along.
　　I got to the Tube and going down the stairs
　　I saw it.
　　A woman saw it too.
　　She said,
　　You've lost a shoe.
　　You've only got one shoe.
　　I thought, I have not.
　　How rude.
　　How dare you.
　　Mind your own.
　　But she was right.
　　I had.
　　I have.
　　It was there, and then it was gone.
　　I've lost a shoe.

I don't know what to do.
　　They're my work shoes.
　　And my weekend shoes.
　　I just buy one pair and then

Wear them out.
I wear them in then
Wear them out.

And it's hot today.
The tarmac is starting to heat up.

*Elaine approaches, sits under the tree. Elaine has been
sleeping rough there for a few nights. She's carrying a
bottle of cider.*

Elaine You've lost a shoe.

Viv Yes.
I've lost a shoe.

Elaine I lost a shoe.
Just before . . .
Yes.
Hard to recall.
It was the shoe first and then . . .
Yes . . . and then . . .
And then I ended up here.
I've only got one shoe, too.
You don't need two.
Shoes.

Viv I do. I've got to go to work.

Elaine Get you.
Buy a new pair.

Viv I don't have enough. I'm up to my limit until next
month.
The limit of the back-up limit.

Elaine My cider's nice and cold.
Feel it.

Viv I don't know what to do.

Elaine Sit here with me if you want.

Viv I can't.

Elaine Sit down and have a think.

Viv I can't sit down.

Elaine Why not?

Viv We'll look the same.
Two women of a certain age, under a tree.
One shoe each, drinking cider.

Elaine You can't have any cider.

Viv It's how it would look.

Elaine You can't have my shoe either.

Viv I don't want your shoe.
Wait. Which foot is it?

Elaine You can't have it.

Viv I don't want it.

Elaine It's nicer than your one.

Viv I don't know what to do.

Elaine Your phone's ringing.

Viv I'm on my way!
No problem.
No problem at all.
I'll be there in half an hour.
It's the trains.
They are a madness.
Yes!
Some of us are just trying to get to work.
And get in the office.
And get stuff done.

Get cracking.
Yes!

Elaine You better go.

Viv I'm going.

Elaine They won't notice you've only got one shoe.

A large floor-to-ceiling window.
   Two pairs of shoes. A man and a woman's.
   Viv's one shoe on its own, adrift.

Viv I told them it's a shoes-off.
   It's a shoes-off sort of house.
   Home.
   So – that works.

I told them.
   You can't argue on the location.
   They're on the roof terrace.
   Having a think.
   Imagining themselves.
   In here.
   Looking out of this window.
   Onto this city.
   I'm happy for them.
   If they think they can make it work.
   I can make it work.
   It's a sale.
   A whale of a sale.

If they make an offer I'll have to talk to
   My boss
   When! they make an offer I'll have to go
   Back
   Across town.
   To the main office.
   To give the fullest possible impression
   That

I am –
I shall hobble proudly towards my
Commission!

They won't make an offer.
He's not in love with her.
I can tell.
He's building up for how to tell her in a way that
Means she tells him.

She looks at her shoe.
She puts on the other pair of shoes. The man's
because they look more comfortable.
And they are. Big, but comfortable.
She takes them off, afraid of being caught.
She puts her foot next to the woman's high-heeled
shoes.

We're the same size.
Isn't that funny.
She's nothing like me.
AT ALL.
I mean she is the,
She's what you want.
Basically.
She's the dream.
I'd want a wife like her.
I need a wife I think.
She doesn't want to be his wife though.
I can tell.
She wants to get a dog.
A puppy dog
And then, you know.
Walk it.
Feed it.
Train it.
Love it.

That's what she wants.
He wants to get promoted.
And be part of things.
It must take ages to wash that window.
Lord.
There's a mark, you know.
A big smear.
Oh no.
A massive smear.
Can't you see?
There's a smear.
A big smear.
Um.

She tiptoes up to reach the smear on the window.
    Uses part of the curtain to clean it.
    Puts the heels on to make her taller.
    She still can't reach.
    She strains, pulls on the curtain.
    The whole rail and two curtains come down.
    The curtain is a massive pile of dark fabric.
    The curtain starts moving.

Curtain She's wearing your shoes.
    She's stolen your shoes.
    Thief!
    Thief!
    Your shoes.
    She's wearing your shoes.

Footsteps coming down from the roof terrace.

Viv Shush.
    Shushhhhh.
    I was going to give them back!

Curtain She's taking them.
    She's running away.

Viv I'm not running away.
  Please.
  Please!
  Shush.
  I wanted to try them on.
  To smudge the smear!
  And see what they felt like
  Shush.
  They were more comfortable than I expected.
  But also a little tight.
  Hard to get off.
  Quickly.
  Hard to yank them off.
  Without scraping the skin.

Office toilets.

Viv I was quite close to making a sale.

Pause.

I'm just so sorry to have let you all down.
    To be disturbing you.
    Letting you down, Lizzie.
    In the office toilets.
    I'm just so tired and so sorry.
    I'm so sorry.
    I feel so sorry I'm almost drunk on sorry.
    Sorry
    Sorry
    Sorry.

I thought maybe you could lend me a pair for my next
    Viewings.
    We started at the same time.
    June, wasn't it?
    And the sun has shone on your sales record.
    Mine a little less
    Dazzling.
    Year on year.
    But we are friends.
    Natterers.
    Colleagues.
    We often nod in the morning.
    We both drink coffee . . .

Silence.

Is no shoes better than one shoe?
　　I can't tell.
　　What do you think?
　　Please tell me.
　　Please share with me?
　　Your thoughts –
　　Would you rather have one shoe or no shoes?
　　There's a clarity in no shoes.
　　The mystery of one shoe is what people
　　Struggle with.
　　Why
　　Why
　　Why
　　One shoe?
　　I lost a shoe. That's why.
　　But it piques curiosity.
　　It invites reproach.

A pair of heeled shoes are slid out from under the door.

Ah.
　　I'll try them but I'm not making any promises.

She takes off her one shoe.
　　Puts on the pair.
　　Walks up and down.
　　Then again.

Ow!
　　They pinch.
　　Across the bridge.
　　Such a pinch.

I can't.
　　I can't.
　　Better to go barefoot.
　　Isn't it?
　　Isn't it?

I feel like I'm letting everyone down.
Letting everybody down.
Again and again.
No matter.
Don't be silly.
Don't be a silly billy.
Don't get down in the dumps.
Buck up.
Buck up, Viv.
It's not even lunchtime.
What's the worst that can happen?
You've only got one shoe.
So what?!
But you lent me your shoes.
That means ever such a –
That fills me with –
All is not –
That kind of generosity gives me hope.
And the strength
To get there.
In time.
And apologise.
Only apologise
For what must be only,
Can only be a mistake on my part.
That I have fallen short.
And I'm not upholding the values
Of our enterprise.
And that is not the kind of worker I am.
That I value my job, it's true!
I need it.
And very often I enjoy the
Cut and thrust of it.
But with one shoe
It's harder to get excited.

It's harder to imagine it's going to get me somewhere.
No matter.
Can't be late.

A café.

Viv A cool glass of water.
   That feels good!
   Refreshing!
   I missed the viewing of course.
   I've let everyone down.
   My foot is.
   Well.
   OUCH.
   It's hurting quite a lot.
   The skin is starting to peel back.
   And to think this was my more attractive foot of the
two.
   Sometimes it's like this city
   Is doing a dance routine.
   Collectively.
   And everyone knows the moves
   Except me!
   I've got two left feet!
   Or two left shoes!
   I should try to dance metaphorically, that is.
   The next time the opportunity arises I will listen for the
inaudible beat
   And dance.
   The inaudible beat and dance.
   The inaudible beat and dance.
   The inaudible beat and dance.
   I can't hear it.
   I can't hear it.

I don't know what I'm supposed to be doing.
What should I do?
What should I do?
I took that lady's shoes!
I took them on.
I should have run fast.
I should have taken them.
How can I keep going with one shoe?
I'm half a being.
Half here.
Half person.
One shoe.
It means something.
What does it mean?
What must they think of me?
What do they think of me?
I'd hate to just be that woman with one shoe.
So good to have a cool glass of water!
Just as the day is warming up!
And at the same time it's like this shoe that I do have is
In mourning.
It's so heavy.
It's missing the other shoe, I'm sure of it.
Poor shoe, that's what I say.
All alone in the city.
Wondering where we've got to!

Police station.

Viv If I found a shoe I would certainly deliver it to the nearest police station.

I'm pretty sure.

Crumbs! I love how these two are speaking!

Crumbs!

I just want to keep hearing them say something.

They've been held up!

Oh! I hate to be late!

Not held up!

Held up! At knife point? No!

I can only apologise on behalf of.

All of us.

On behalf of this city.

What did they take?

Everything!

Oh poor things. Look at them!

They must think we're desperate!

They must think we're falling apart at the seams!

We are good people, you know!

We're not all on the breadline!

Some of us can still afford to have some dignity.

Not all of us are criminals!

There are some of course who can't control themselves

But it's not who we are!

We have honour!

We have a range cooker for a start. I think that's a sign

If you needed one for respectability.

Holding up and stealing from American tourists!

36

A family of four.
Two teens in baseball caps.
Him in his long lens, he must have clung tight to that.
Her in her pumps and zippy pouch.
We should feel lucky they are still coming here.
Welcome!
You are welcome!
I have lost a shoe! It wasn't stolen, I'm fairly sure.
I'm here to check if it's been handed in.
No?
I've lost my right shoe. It's identical to the left.
You haven't received a right shoe?
Sure?
How odd!
I hope they say something else in American now!
The child at least.
I want to hear all the words twang!
Silence!
They hate us, for being so pathetic.
It takes real fortitude to be in essence and spirit middle
class in this town.
It takes real guts to keep it together –
I hope you can enjoy the rest of your holiday!
How nice to be on holiday!
I don't even remember the last time I took holiday!
I get twenty-four days a year but I'm always too afraid
to ask for them.
So I don't take them. Just the bank holidays.

I don't want them to have another reason to hate me.
To let me go.
It's all so fragile!
Don't go on holiday!
Don't have another baby!
Don't sneeze.
Hold on to your job.

It feels like we're right on the edge.
We're not, of course.
We're fine.
I'm being silly.
We're just as it should be.
Nothing's changed.
All is well.

Shop.

Viv They are trying my card in the machine again.
   Give it a good rub on the dress.
   She's incredibly well dressed for
   Sales personnel.
   And a swipe in the machine.
   A tap.
   A touch.
   Whatever works.
   I shouldn't have bought that juice just now, it's tipped
my card over the edge.
   This is a lovely pair of shoes!
   Such good value!
   They ought to last at least forever.
   They won't.
   But the *idea* is that they will.
   The *idea* is worth paying for.
   The best bit is that there are TWO!
   Who would have thought that two shoes
   Could be so important!
   It's the difference between –
   Well –
   It makes a difference!
   It makes a difference!
   One shoe and you look like –
   Well!
   You look like something you're not!
   Two shoes and you're normal.
   Oh sweet normal.

What an ordeal!
I'll put them both on.
To see.
Yes, sweet TWO!
Sweet PAIR.
Look at me!
Look at me!
I can really walk in these.
Oh no.
A bit of blood.
How embarrassing!
A bit of blood from my foot.
On these lovely new shoes.
Don't look at me!
Don't look at my shoes!
I'm gathering up my things.
I'm taking my card.
I'm walking out the door.
Two shoes and it's so easy to run!
It's so easy to move.
I can run so fast like this.
I can!
A man jogging past me.
He smells of fresh laundry!
Heaven!
What a life he must have!
What a wife!
I want a wife!

A tree.

Elaine And you unwrap the paper.
  And inside the paper is nothing.
  But instead of feeling upset.
  You start to laugh and you unwrap it and you say –
nothing!
  You get a sweet wrapper, you unwrap it and no sweet.
  Nothing!

Viv I don't want to unwrap nothing.

Elaine Why not?
  It's good.
  You're fine without anything sometimes.

Viv Of course.
  I just mean.
  I don't want to have to do that.
  I find it really depressing.
  I would get really depressed.

Elaine I've hardly had anything today. I'm dehydrated.
  Look, my lips are chapped.
  I can tell you stole those.

Viv Hardly!

Elaine You did.
  I can tell.

Viv Hardly!
  I have a car
  And a mortgage

And childcare
And thread-count linen.
I didn't steal these.

Elaine I know.
But you did.

And your feet are all bloody.

Viv It's not often I feel sorry for myself
But heavens.
Heavens!
It's so unfair!
What am I going to do?!
Give your shoe to me and you can have these ones.

Elaine No.
I'd prefer not.

Viv Please.

Elaine She begs!

Viv Please.

Elaine No.
I don't want to.
For lots of reasons.
No.
You should take them off, though.
Because you did steal them.
And you might get caught.
You should give them to me.

Viv They're mine.
Get off.
Get off me.
Get off.

Home.

Viv Damp laundry!
      That terrible smell.
      The smell of nowhere to put a tumble dryer.
      I ought to put these clothes in the wash.

On the way back I had a sudden memory.
      A memory of giving birth and
      The pain and the loneliness of it.
      And trying so hard to bring something into being
      And thinking it might never happen
      And it was just a terrible dream
      And then I realised it's
      Our little one's birthday.
      Our prince. Last year we were flat
      Broke so we gave him a kind
      Of retro tea party.
      And it was quite affordable but
      Then Kenny bought him a scooter
      With all the paraphernalia and
      He was so happy
      But it was very expensive.
      We've got no money but we're still
      In Waitrose twice a day.
      Kenny will be home with him soon, I don't
      Know what to do.
      I don't know what to do.
      My body felt like a cloud after birth.
      It still does.

I'm a cloud floating around.
Nothing I touch even
Notices I'm here.

Kenny and Child are looking at a large piece of screwed-up paper.

Viv Open it!
Don't just stand there!
Open it!
Open it!

The Child opens it.

Nothing!
Nothing!
Isn't it wonderful!
Nothing!
There's nothing in there!
Nothing!
Doesn't it feel good!
Nothing!
Nothing!
There's nothing there!
How wonderful.
Let me screw it up again.
Wait.
Let me wrap up nothing again.
Let me wrap it up.
There.
Try again.
Nothing.

Kenny He gets it. Nothing.

Viv Yes.
   Nothing.
   Can you be happy?
   Is he happy?
   Can he be happy with nothing?
   Kenny?
   I could be I could be, Kenny.
   I don't need anything.
   I don't need anything.

Kenny Did you buy new shoes?

Viv Doorbell.
   Get the door will you, Kenny.
   Get the door will you.
   Get the door.
   Who is it?
   Tell them we're having a birthday.
   Tell them to leave us alone.

Police station.

Viv Oh no! The poor American family are still here!
What a nightmare!
I'm so sorry!
I can only apologise on behalf of all of us.
I'm here because I accidentally walked out of a shop
In a pair of shoes.
I think!
Or perhaps a worse crime yet to be revealed to me.
I'm sure I'm guilty of something.
She was incredibly annoying.
It's starting to sink in now.
What a terrible thing to have done.
I can't quite believe it.
I don't know what a person is supposed to do
In this situation.
I don't know what I'm supposed to do.
I suppose they'll call me 'Killer Viv'.
What a terrible person.
I've sunk so low.
She was a person too.
Who was?
I haven't done anything, have I?
Or have I?
The shoes?
All my frustrations I just let it all out.
That's not fair.
That's not right.
It's absolutely correct I should be punished.

But take mercy, I'm a mother.
I'm a mother and a wife!
They'll come out and call my name in a moment.
Take my fingerprints.
Fill me in on why I'm here.
Criminal that I am.
The blood on my clothes too.
It's not blood!
They'll know everything!
Heavens!
There is blood.
From my foot!
Yes!
There's a reasonable explanation for everything.
I don't know why I let it all get on top of me.
I haven't done anything wrong.
Not on purpose.
I'm a worker.
That's me.

Home.

Viv So dark!
  Kenny?
  Kenny?
  Kenny?

I lost it.
  The buckle.
  I had two shoes
  And then suddenly it was only one.
  And then I accidentally stole a pair from Russell and
Bromley.
  And then I had to give them back
  Because the police asked me to.
  They were very polite about it.
  They understood it was an accident.
  I had to limp home in one shoe.
  The sole of my other foot is ripped raw.
  I never knew how much this city hurt me until today.
  How fragile we are.
  I get so scared about how close we live
  To not being able to live.

It's incredibly hard, isn't it.
  To stay afloat.
  It's incredibly hard not to sink to the bottom.
  My foot is so sore.
  I don't have anything to wear tomorrow.
  I still don't have another pair.
  I don't know how I've let this happen.

I don't know how I've only got one shoe.
I'm not a person this can be true of.
I'm not a one-shoe person.
I'm a two-shoe person.
I have two shoes.
I need two shoes.
The world doesn't work for one shoe.
I don't know what to do.
I don't know what to do.
I can't go to work tomorrow.
I'll need to tell Kenny I can't go, until I can sort myself out.
I can't go there again with one shoe.
Stop actually
I've done it again.
I've allowed myself to stoop low into despair.
Silly! Silly old mare.
It's not all bad!
Kenny?
I'm sure the only reason I would have to go to work tomorrow.
His meeting.
I'm sure it went well.
We are lucky people!
I just need a day to get myself
Back on track.

Bedroom. Night-time.
   Viv and Child are in the bed.

Viv He knows today hasn't started yet.
   That we are to wait.
   We are waiting for the day.
   We are still asleep.
   Kenny's got the right idea.
   On the sofa.
   He will have a tremendously productive day now
tomorrow.
   We will feel rotten
   And sunken with the lack of sleep.
   But no matter.
   There's a kind of high to being so low on sleep.
   We are asleep.
   I will wake us soon and we'll get to the day.

Go and get Daddy.
   Go, will you.
   Off you go.
   Now.
   Now please.
   Now.

   The Child goes.
      After a long time Kenny arrives.
      He stands in the doorway wanting to know what she can possibly want.
      She pulls back the sheet. She's bleeding heavily.

Oh.
    I was.
    I wasn't sure.
    But how lovely for me.
    For us.
    How wonderful.
    To have been.
    A few weeks perhaps.
    A miscarriage. A miscarriage of justice.
    It will be alright.
    I shall park this.
    And
    Come back to it.
    And the admin of it.
    Don't worry.
    Don't worry.
    Don't worry, Kenny, go back to bed.
    You will only cry.

    He waits to see if she is sure.

Better really that I'm not.
    Breaking in two it feels.
    Am I?
    Am I whole?
    I have to go to work tomorrow.
    Better get some sleep.
    Got to get back to work.
    One of us has to!
    One of us has to keep it together.
    No matter.
    Nighty-night.

    He goes.

Night-night.
    It's a work night.

Bedroom. Morning, under the bed.

Viv Under here! What hidden glory!
  Under here!
  Under the bed!
  Oh I could move in here.
  It's incredibly moving.
  It's a real something.
  Kenny!
  Kenny!
  Come and look under here!
  I thought my old trainers might be here.
  But we got rid of almost everything when the baby
came.
  No room for spare shoes.
  I'll be late again I should think.
  I could stay under here all day though.
  Here's where real life is.
  Here's where the dreams went
  Here's where we put everything away.
  Oh heaven!
  I want to move in under here and
  Commune with all our crap.
  All I need to do is get out there and make it work
  For me.
  Poor foot.
  You're going to get it again all over again.
  I had a rich friend once
  She used to joy
  Truly joy in the everyday experience.

She really took the time
To weep at the trees
And to consider the texture of the road underfoot.
Now foot it's all on you.
You've got to take it
And pretend it's a kind of poetry.
We can try and pass it off as if
We are wealthy and eccentric.
That this is a sort of joke.
We can try and act humorous.
We can try and not look like
It hurts.
With a kind of murderous stabbing sensation.
We must try and look poetic
About it.
Look, the toes quiver.
I don't know how to force my foot outside into the
humiliation.
Of hobbling towards the Tube.
I don't know what to do.
I've only got one shoe.
I want someone to help me even though
I don't deserve help.
I am certain there are others who need it more.
I don't know what to do.
I've only got one shoe.

Office toilets.

Viv I tried to explain.
    Yes.
    I am wearing one shoe.
    Again.
    For the second day running.
    But in no way is this a reflection on my respect for my job, the company or its clients.
    I hold all these in the utmost
    High regard.
    But I only have one shoe.
    I tried to get another shoe.
    But I only have one shoe.
    Why can't I just do my job
    With one shoe?
    If only just for today.
    Let me have one shoe.
    There is nothing I can do.
    My foot is in considerable pain.
    The other shoe
    The remaining shoe
    Is an excellent shoe.
    It's just bad luck.
    That one shoe should break.
    A buckle.
    And leave me a shoe short of normal.
    Kenny will be devastated.
    He is out of work as of yesterday.
    And now me too.

How quickly we have sunk to the bottom.
There will be a safety net surely!
We will not disappear.
The world is waiting to see what interesting things
We will do.
The world needs us at our best.
Our photographs and our debit-card purchases.
The world is hungry for
Our activities and our ideas.
We must not disappoint
Our audience.
We've got so much to offer.
We weren't just plodding along.
We were really trying to contribute.
We have been participating.
Just like we are meant to.
We are workers.
We have been working.
Working.

A breeze.
In through the toilet window.
Heaven!
New thoughts flood into the brain
After a reviving breeze like that.
What a toilet window.
How lucky I am!

If I could wish for anything now, anything
In the world I would wish for –
Um.
I
Um.
I.
Anything.
No limitations.

Only limited
By
Imagination.
That
Mine is still.
Breathing.
Of course.
I
Um.
Anything.
If I could have anything.
A miracle.
The light of luck shining down on me and mine!
I can have anything I want!
Anything!
Anything!
I know.
I know.
Of course.
Shoe.
My shoe.

Street.

Viv Lucy, it's me. I'm sorry I didn't call you back
  After you called me back
  After I called you back that time
  After we got cut off
  And you told me that
  He'd told you what he'd done.
  And I never had time
  To respond
  And to tell you how bad it made me
  Feel for you
  And that I'm sorry
  It happened to you.
  I feel very –
  I didn't know who to.
  Can you?
  Are you?
  What if we just keep missing each other
  Until the end of time.
  Nothing will ever get
  Spoken of.
  Nothing will be noted.
  You are my witness.
  To what is happening.
  Call me back.
  When you.
  Can.
  No rush.

Was just calling to catch.
Up.

A fence.

Viv There's a shoe on a fence post.
   Just sitting there.
   It looks exactly like my shoe.
   Just sitting there.
   Aren't you?
   Worlds fall apart!
   Whole universes expire, and then
   Reunited at last!
   Miracle!
   A little too late.
   Too little too late.
   But not too late!
   Never too late.
   We can agree to say.
   Never irredeemable.
   Never not reachable from the brink.
   Were you always here?
   My foot's too swollen now, I can't get it on.
   I can't get it back in.
   It's misshapen now.
   Whoever heard of that.
   I'll take it home and see if Kenny can help me squeeze
my foot back inside.
   Even if it makes me scream with pain.
   I need to get my foot back in the shoe.
   I have two shoes.
   I should be elated and overjoyed.

I need to shove it back in.
I can do it myself.
If I don't mind the pressure on the flesh.
I can feel it.
Unimaginable pain.
And I'm part of it all again.
I'm part of things.
I'm back in the swing.
Of it.
I was really on the outside for a moment there.
But it was fleeting.
I'm ready to participate.
I'm ready to work.
Never doubt my commitment.
Such a shoe!
The buckle is flapping in the wind.
No matter.
I can hobble still.
One leg slower than the other.
It works!
All is well!
All is well!
It works.
It works.
I can work.
The wheel turns.
The grist mills.
The engine purrs.
I can hobble.
I can work.
I have two shoes.
It hurts though.
It hurts.
It hurts.

But it's alright.
It's alright.
It's alright that it hurts.

A tree.
   The ache and crack of branches moving.

Tree When I see their faces.
   Walking past.
   I want to think yes.
   This is.
   This is what I've been looking for.
   Rustle
   Rustle
   Rustle.
   I watch them
   Scuttle
   Rustle
   Rustle
   Rustle.
   Blotchy skin.
   Cut up
   Creased up.
   Rustle.
   Breaking
   Breaking into little bits.
   Right at the end.
   Of their.
   Rustle
   Rustle.
   Ready to start again.
   I hear them speak.
   And I wonder how they
   Keep on

Clawing.
Clawing on.
Rustle
Rustle
Rustle
Rustle.
To get somewhere
To get something of nothing.
Nothing of something.
I hear them speak.
Rustle.
Their hollow little squeaky voices.
Rustle.
Still so full of hope.
I wait for the wind to pick up.
So I can't hear
And then I don't have to listen.